# A Patchwork Notebook

JINNY BEYER

Breckling Press

This book was set in Walbaum Book and Didot by Bartko Design, Inc.
Editorial direction by Anne Knudsen
Art direction, cover and interior design by Kim Bartko, Bartko Design, Inc.

The antique needlework illustrations opposite and on pages 18 and 88 were originally published in *La Mode Illustrée*, issues dated from 1871 to 1876; the diagrams on pages 81, 101, and 113 are by Kandy Peterson; the quilting illustrations on page 108 are from *The Quilt Fair Comes to You Aunt Martha*, 1932; the illustration on page 7 is from *Godey's Lady's Book*, 1849; the illustration on page 54 is from *The Mary Frances Sewing Book for Girls* by Jane Eayre Fryer; and the illustration on page 80 is from *Encyclopedia of Needlework* by Therese de Dillmont; the quilting illustrations on pages 42, 50, and 60 are from *The Romance of the Patchwork Quilt in America* by Carrie A. Hall and Rose Kretsinger; the photographs on pages 30 and 92 are by Sharon Hoogstraten. All other illustrations are from the collection of Jinny Beyer.

Published by Breckling Press
283 Michigan St.
Elmhurst, IL 60126 USA

Printed and bound in China
International Standard Book Number: 0-9721-2186-2

# Dedication

*A reason many of us make quilts is to create loving memories. What better way to keep those memories alive than to write down your thoughts as your quilt comes together?*

# *Introduction*

IDEAS FOR PATTERNS AND DESIGNS pop into our minds at surprising
moments. Perhaps at church you suddenly see something in the stained
glass window that you never noticed before, or quite by accident you come
across an unusual floor or tile pattern. We never know when inspirations
for our next patchwork designs will come to us. What better way to keep
track of all those ideas than by jotting them down? This journal was
created for just such a purpose. Small enough to keep in a purse and with
a binding that protects the pages, *A Patchwork Notebook* will quickly
become a constant companion. Not only is there lots of room to write
down your thoughts, but the grid papers in the back make it easy to sketch
out patchwork designs as soon as ideas come to you.

I often recommend to new quilters that they keep a journal as an
ongoing diary of a particular quilt project. Perhaps you will use your
notebook to keep track of specifics, such as colors, fabrics, patterns, or the
evolution of a project. Or you may choose to use your journal simply to
store thoughts or memories of your day-to-day life while you work on a
certain quilt. You might even keep a companion diary to gift to a loved one,
along with a finished quilt.

Sewing creates memories—and not just for the maker of the quilt, but
for family members or friends who may have sat and chatted with the
quilter while the work was being stitched. Loving memories are part of

the quilting tradition. I can look at each and every one of the quilts I have made and recall images of what was happening in my life and in the lives of those around me during the time a particular quilt was being stitched. Often it is the quilts that have the most pieces and perhaps the more involved techniques that hold the strongest memories of all.

　　If you keep a companion journal as you quilt, when each project is complete, you not only have a record for your own reference, but you have notes that will be cherished by future generations—just as they cherish the quilts you make.

Jinny Beyer

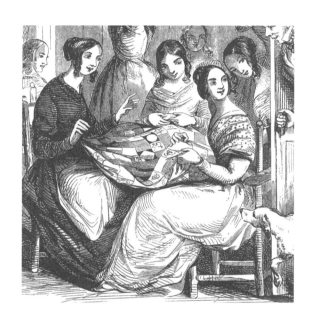

*"Then you thread a needle and settle comfortably in your chair. The needle runs easily back and forth through soft cloth while nerves relax and useless worries fade away. Smoothing out a finished block, you have a pleasant sense of achievement. You are making a thing of beauty that generations will come to prize."*

ROSE WILDER LANE,
*The Woman's Day Book of American Needlework, 1964*

**DATE** _____

**DATE** _____

**DATE** _____

"*I know how to knot my thread; I'll show you, after I get this needle threaded—now! . . . I wind the thread around the tip of the first finger of my left hand. . . . I press it with my thumb and roll the thread downward to the tip end of my finger—so! . . . Then I bring the second finger over the thread on the thumb. . . . Then draw the thread tight with the right hand as I hold it.*"

JANE EAYRE FRYER
*The Mary Frances Sewing Book for Girls,* 1913

DATE _____

........................................................................................................
........................................................................................................
........................................................................................................
........................................................................................................
........................................................................................................
........................................................................................................
........................................................................................................
........................................................................................................
........................................................................................................
........................................................................................................
........................................................................................................
........................................................................................................
........................................................................................
........................................................................................
........................................................................................
........................................................................................
........................................................................................
........................................................................................

## TIP

Quilting is what you want it to be—there
are no hard-and-fast rules. Practice, find a
rhythm that is comfortable for you, then
begin a project. Enjoy those moments when
you quietly stitch, reflect, and create your
own special quilt.

DATE _____

DATE _____

*"To begin with, I want to say something as trite as it is important, and that is, 'Use the very best materials that you can afford for any and all handwork.' Extravagance is never smart, but good quilt materials are not expensive. It's the sleazy ones, unreliable dyes and starched cloth that prove expensive in the end."*

RUBY SHORT McKIM

*One Hundred and One Patchwork Patterns, 1931*

## DATE _____

........................................................................................
........................................................................................
........................................................................................
........................................................................................
........................................................................................
........................................................................................
........................................................................................
........................................................................................
........................................................................................
........................................................................................
........................................................................................
........................................................................................
........................................................................................

## TIP

When selecting fabrics, seek to achieve a good balance in the scale and type of print. Choose large-, medium-, and small-scale prints as well as a variety of designs — florals, plaids, checks, or geometrics. Also, try to have a good balance between tonal and multi-colored prints.

**DATE** _____

DATE _____

"Opinions vary much as to the age when a little girl may safely be instructed in sewing; and each mother will be guided in this matter by the nature of her own child, some little ones being sufficiently advanced to commence at three years of age."

Cassell's Household Guide to Every Department of Practical Life, Volume IV, circa 1875

## DATE _____

....................................................................................................................

....................................................................................................................

....................................................................................................................

....................................................................................................................

....................................................................................................................

....................................................................................................................

....................................................................................................................

....................................................................................................................

....................................................................................................................

....................................................................................................................

....................................................................................................................

....................................................................................................................

....................................................................................................................

....................................................................................................................

....................................................................................................................

## TIP

There is no need to cut out all the pieces
you need for a quilt before you begin
sewing. I prefer to cut just enough pieces
to make a start on my first blocks or the
first portion of a design. Not only does this
break up the tedious task of cutting, but it
allows extra flexibility — if I am not satisfied
with my fabric selections in those first
blocks, it is easy to make a change.

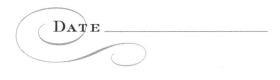

DATE _____

DATE _____

"*Piecing a quilt top is not such a formidable task. Really a knowledge of plain sewing, accuracy and neatness are all that are required to add to that desire to make it yourself.*"

RUBY SHORT McKIM

*One Hundred and One Patchwork Patterns*, 1931

## DATE _____

...........................................................................
...........................................................................
...........................................................................
...........................................................................
...........................................................................
...........................................................................
...........................................................................
...........................................................................
...........................................................................
...........................................................................
...........................................................................
...........................................................................
...........................................................................
...........................................................................

## TIP

My color system is guided by four basic
principles. First, whatever colors you select,
make sure you have several shades of each.
Second, always have one color that is darker
than the general range you are working with
(the deep dark). Third, always have a color
that is a brighter shade (the accent). Finally,
make sure to include some neutrals, such as
brown, gray, taupe, or khaki.

DATE _____

DATE _____

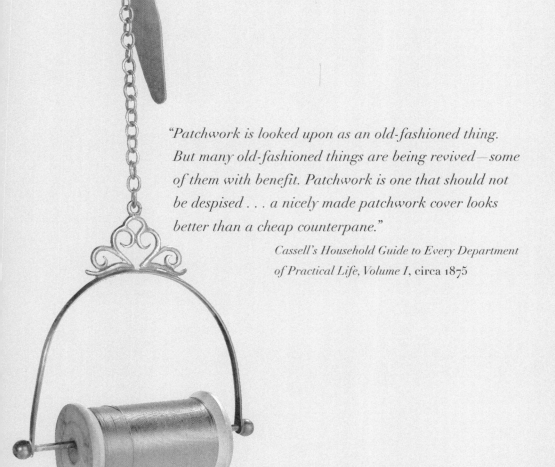

"*Patchwork is looked upon as an old-fashioned thing. But many old-fashioned things are being revived — some of them with benefit. Patchwork is one that should not be despised . . . a nicely made patchwork cover looks better than a cheap counterpane.*"

Cassell's Household Guide to Every Department
of Practical Life, Volume I, circa 1875

## DATE _____

..................................................................................................
..................................................................................................
..................................................................................................
..................................................................................................
..................................................................................................
..................................................................................................
..................................................................................................
..................................................................................................
..................................................................................................
..................................................................................................
..................................................................................................
..................................................................................................
..................................................................................................

## TIP

When sewing a dark piece to a light one,
use thread of the darker color or close to it.
The stitches are more apt to show when
using light-colored thread. Never use a
thread that is lighter in color than either of
the two pieces you are sewing, or the
stitches will show.

DATE _____

DATE

"'Why spend so much time and labor making new quilts and
worrying about designs when you already have a number which
are never used?' Perhaps it is for the same reason which prompts
the planting of flowers in the alley . . . or the landscaping of our
gardens in places seen only by the few; because of our love for
beauty and regard for order in everyday living. It is in us and most
come forth and become a material artistic expression."

CARRIE A HALL AND ROSE G KRETSINGER,
*The Romance of the Patchwork Quilt in America*, 1935

......................................................................................................................

......................................................................................................................

......................................................................................................................

......................................................................................................................

......................................................................................................................

......................................................................................................................

......................................................................................................................

......................................................................................................................

......................................................................................................................

## TIP

Whether you work by hand or machine, resist the urge to press your work after completing each seam or even each block. Too much pressing distorts bias edges, spoiling the shape of the finished block. I recommend placing the finished block right side up on top of a large, fluffy towel, then ironing the block from right to left. I let the seams go where they want to rather than force them in one direction, which sometimes creates bulk at intersections. The only exception is when joining very light fabrics with darker ones. I press the seams toward the darker fabric so that it doesn't show through the lighter one.

DATE _____

DATE _____

"'The great object of all instruction' —says a recent writer— 'is to strengthen the mind, and form the character. Even needlework, humble as the employment may appear, may be made conducive to this end. When it is intelligently taught, the mind is employed as well as the fingers; powers of calculation are drawn out, habits of neatness acquired, and the taste and judgment cultivated in a way which eminently fits women for the higher branches of service, and enables them to fill even those the most menial with credit to themselves, and comfort to their employers.'"

*Cassell's Household Guide to Every Department of Practical Life, Volume II*, circa 1890

....................................................................................................
....................................................................................................
....................................................................................................
....................................................................................................
....................................................................................................
....................................................................................................
....................................................................................................
....................................................................................................
....................................................................................................
....................................................................................................

## TIP

Value placement—the use of dark, medium, and light values—is one of the most important elements of quilt design. I complete all pattern design in black and white, either on the computer or with pencil and paper. I make a line drawing, photocopy it several times, then fill in with different light, medium, and dark values on each copy, arranging and rearranging the quilt layout as I work. Only when I am satisfied with value placements do I go to my fabric stash.

DATE _____

DATE _____

" . . . for it was the quilting rather than the piecing—difficult and exacting as this was in many instances—that required the last degree of needlework attainment . . . Quilting was an accomplishment into which went not only technique but feeling."

RUTH E. FINLEY
*Old Patchwork Quilts and the Women Who Made Them,* 1929

DATE _____

........................................................................................................................

........................................................................................................................

........................................................................................................................

........................................................................................................................

........................................................................................................

........................................................................................................

........................................................................................................

........................................................................................................

........................................................................................................

........................................................................................................

........................................................................................................................

........................................................................................................................

........................................................................................................................

........................................................................................................................

........................................................................................................................

DATE _____

DATE

"As the result of many years spent over the quilting frame, some quilters acquire an unusual dexterity in handling the needle, and occasionally one is encountered who can quilt as well with one hand as with the other."

MARIE D. WEBSTER
*Quilts: Their Story & How to Make Them*, 1915

**DATE** _____

**TIP**

To understand how to
*shade* colors together, think
of a rainbow, where it is
impossible to tell where one
color ends and the other
begins. Your palette of fabrics
should achieve the same
smooth blending of colors.

DATE _____

DATE _____

"*When the girl was promised, and the wedding day drew near, the patchwork top was sewn, or completed if it had been started earlier. It really looked lovely—not like everyday quilts at all, for a definite pattern had perhaps naturally followed on the definite color scheme. Well, then, the quilting must be worthy of such a fine top!*"

AGNES M. MIALL
*Patchwork Old and New*, 1937

## DATE _____

...............................................................................................................................

...............................................................................................................................

...............................................................................................................................

...............................................................................................................................

...............................................................................................................................

...............................................................................................................................

...............................................................................................................................

...............................................................................................................................

...............................................................................................................................

...............................................................................................................................

## TIP

I never mark seam allowances on my fabrics. I consider this not just a waste of time but prone to inaccuracy. Instead, I cut all pieces to the full size of the template, including seam allowance. When I'm ready to sew, I pin the pieces together at the points where the seam allowances will cross. I then eyeball a ¼" seam allowance and sew from pin to pin. I have taught hand piecing to hundreds of students and firmly believe that, with practice, anyone can eyeball a ¼" seam allowance with accuracy.

DATE

DATE _____

T he first time she ever helped me was with my wedding dress"

"'Ah, my dear, you've not been lonely,' said Grandma, '. . . You've been playing with my old fashioned sewing bird, I see. Many a year this pretty little beak has held Grandma's long seams and hems while she sewed them . . . the first time she ever helped me,' she added softly, 'was with my wedding dress.'"

JANE EAYRE FRYER
*The Mary Frances Sewing Book for Girls*, 1913

........................................................................................................................................................

........................................................................................................................................................

........................................................................................................................................................

........................................................................................................................................................

........................................................................................................................................................

........................................................................................................................................................

........................................................................................................................................................

........................................................................................................................................................

........................................................................................................................................................

## TIP

When sewing by hand, it is important to maintain the proper tension on the fabric in order to keep stitches neat and even. I make sure that the index fingers at the back of the piece are no more than about ⅛" apart and that they constantly pull away from each other to create tension on the fabric. Without good tension, it is hard to get into a rhythm—as soon as the tension is relaxed, there is slack in the cloth and the seam starts to get crooked.

DATE _____

DATE _____

DATE _____

DATE

"*[This quilt] is an outburst of joy. . . . At the sight of it, every face brightens. How can . . . mere pieces of cloth sewed together have this power to lift the human spirit? No one can explain this; it is the mystery of art.*"

ROSE WILDER LANE
*The Woman's Day Book of American Needlework*, 1964

........................................................................................................................

........................................................................................................................

........................................................................................................................

........................................................................................................................

........................................................................................................................

........................................................................................................................

........................................................................................................................

........................................................................................................................

........................................................................................................................

........................................................................................................................

## TIP

There are few skills as valuable to quilters as the ability to draft designs. While there are thousands of ready-made patterns available, rarely will you find one that is exactly right for the quilt you have in mind. Most often, the blocks or borders are not the size you want them to be, or the pattern itself may no be quite what you envisage. Being able to draft your own patterns in whatever size you choose allows you the freedom to make your quilts exactly how you want them to be.

DATE _____

"*Ninety nine percent of all pieced quilts represent the working out of geometrical designs, often so intricate that their effective handling reflects most creditably on the supposedly non-mathematical sex.*"

RUTH E. FINLEY

*Old Patchwork Quilts and the Women Who Made Them*, 1929

# DATE _____

.............................................................................................................................................
.............................................................................................................................................
.............................................................................................................................................
.............................................................................................................................................
.............................................................................................................................................
.............................................................................................................................................
.............................................................................................................................................
.............................................................................................................................................
.............................................................................................................................................
.............................................................................................................................................
.............................................................................................................
.............................................................................................................
.............................................................................................................
.............................................................................................................
.............................................................................................................

## TIP

The darker or brighter the
color, the more inclined the
fabric is to bleed when
washed. Also, the hotter
the water, the more the
dyes will run. Wash all dark
or intense colors in cold
water to prevent bleeding.

DATE _____

DATE

*"The arranging of patterns to make a good and well-balanced design calls for much ingenuity on the part of the worker. A few designs carefully arranged are much more effective than a mass of different ones showing no forethought."*

BEATRICE SCOTT
*The Craft of Quilting,* 1935

.....................................................................................................................................................................

.....................................................................................................................................................................

.....................................................................................................................................................................

.....................................................................................................................................................................

.....................................................................................................................................................................

.....................................................................................................................................................................

.....................................................................................................................................................................

.....................................................................................................................................................................

## TIP

Is it best to begin stitching at the edge of the pieces or at the seam allowances? The answer is that sometimes you can begin at the edges and sometimes you must begin at the place where the seam allowances cross. Whenever the stitching results in an *inward* angle the stitching *must* begin at the place where the seam allowances cross. Where the stitching results in an *outward* angle the stitching can begin at the edges, perhaps lending a little more stability. For straight line sewing where no angles are involved, I usually stitch all the way to the end.

DATE

DATE _____

*"Many of the scrap quilts . . . are very pretty when made from gay pieces — carefully blended — of the various shades of a single color. The stars in the design . . . are made of a great variety of different patterns of pink calico, yet the blending is so good that the effect is greatly heightened by the multiplicity of shades."*

MARIE D. WEBSTER

*Quilts: Their Story & How to Make Them,* 1915

....................................................................................................................

....................................................................................................................

....................................................................................................................

....................................................................................................................

....................................................................................................................

....................................................................................................................

....................................................................................................................

....................................................................................................................

....................................................................................................

....................................................................................................

....................................................................................................

....................................................................................................

....................................................................................................

....................................................................................................

....................................................................................................

## TIP

When hand stitching, never sew seams
down into the line of stitching. Always
leave the seams free. This will help create
a more secure joining of the seams to the
next piece and, when sewing several points
together, will help to create neat, sharp
points that come together perfectly.

DATE _____

DATE

*"Occasionally modern patchwork is made by machine. But such short seams are rather fiddling work done in this way and to my mind much of its charm lies in its restful handwork opportunities."*

AGNES M. MIALL
*Patchwork Old and New,* 1937

......................................................................................................................

......................................................................................................................

......................................................................................................................

......................................................................................................................

......................................................................................................................

......................................................................................................................

......................................................................................................................

......................................................................................................................

......................................................................................................................

......................................................................................................................

## TIP

When hand stitching, work with as small a needle as you are able. While it may be easier to thread a larger needle, it is much more difficult to get it to glide with ease through fabrics. Working with smaller needles may be awkward at first, but will reward you will neat, even stitches. Buy a package of needles with multiple sizes. Begin with the size that is most comfortable for you, and work your way down to a Betweens size 10 or 11.

DATE _____

DATE

*"The stitching itself may be described as a running or darning stitch, not a stab stitch. The worker must keep her left hand under the work and must prick her finger every time the needle comes through the quilt, so as to ensure a perfect stitch on both sides of the work, and no one should be able to say on which side the quilting was done. It stands to reason that the thicker the quilt the coarser the stitching, but evenness counts for higher points than small stitches."*

BEATRICE SCOTT
*The Craft of Quilting*, 1935

## DATE _____

........................................................................................................

........................................................................................................

........................................................................................................

........................................................................................................

........................................................................................................

........................................................................................................

........................................................................................................

........................................................................................................

........................................................................................................

..............................................................

..............................................................

..............................................................

..............................................................

..............................................................

..............................................................

..............................................................

..............................................................

## TIP

When hand piecing, here's how to get rid of unwanted knots in the thread. Hold the end of the thread that was passed through the needle, then slide the needle down the thread all the way to the sewing. Let go of the end of the thread and slowly pull the needle back up. As the needle comes up, the thread will untwist.

DATE _____

DATE _____

"To sit down with paper and pencil and try to figure out how to cut a square of cloth into eight diamonds which, when joined together, will form a perfectly matched star of a definitely desired size, is a task that the modern girl just out of college may well hesitate to undertake. But great-great-grandmother did not waste time bothering her head over any such problem. Many years before the kindergarten was dreamed of, she employed one of its elementary practices, with the aid of scrap bag and scissors. Diamond patches are the most ingenious of the results she achieved."

RUTH E. FINLEY
*Old Patchwork Quilts and the Women Who Made Them*, 1929

........................................................................................................

........................................................................................................

........................................................................................................

........................................................................................................

........................................................................................................

........................................................................................................

........................................................................................................

........................................................................................................

........................................................................................................

........................................................................................................

........................................................................................................

........................................................................................................

........................................................................................

........................................................................................

........................................................................................

........................................................................................

........................................................................................

## TIP

When piecing by hand,
make a small backstitch
each time you pull the
thread through. This gives
extra stability to the seam.

DATE _____

DATE _____

*"We hear so much about this jazz-age being hard on the nerves. Quilt making is the ideal prescription for high-tension nerves. It is soothing and there is no exercise can equal that of really creating something with the hands. And later the product of these hands may be handed down as treasured heirlooms."*

CARRIE A HALL AND ROSE G KRETSINGER
*The Romance of the Patchwork Quilt in America, 1935*

DATE _____

....................................................................................................

....................................................................................................

....................................................................................................

....................................................................................................

....................................................................................................

....................................................................................................

....................................................................................................

....................................................................................................

....................................................................................................

...............................................................

...............................................................

...............................................................

...............................................................

...............................................................

...............................................................

## TIP

When sewing rows of triangles together,
such as in a border, don't break the thread,
but just keep going up the side of one
triangle and down the next in sort of a
zig-zag stitching pattern.

DATE _____

DATE _____

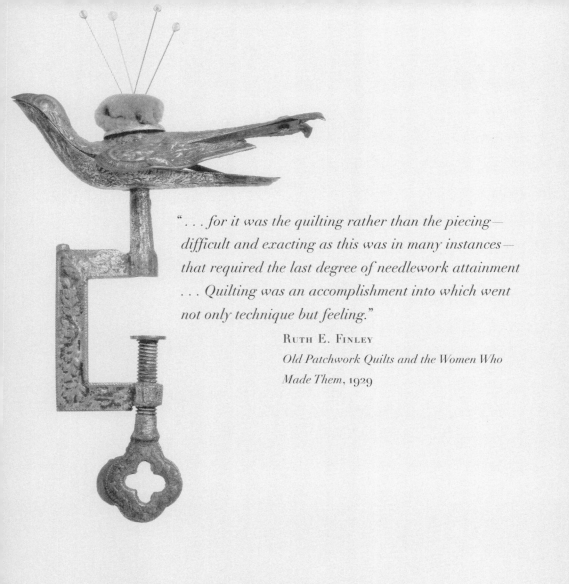

"... for it was the quilting rather than the piecing—
difficult and exacting as this was in many instances—
that required the last degree of needlework attainment
... Quilting was an accomplishment into which went
not only technique but feeling."

RUTH E. FINLEY
*Old Patchwork Quilts and the Women Who
Made Them, 1929*

## DATE _____

.........................................................................................................................................

.........................................................................................................................................

.........................................................................................................................................

.........................................................................................................................................

.........................................................................................................................................

.........................................................................................................................................

.........................................................................................................................................

## TIP

When you first cut curved pieces from fabric for a pattern like *Drunkard's Path*, it often seems that the concave piece on top is too big to fit into the other piece. This is just an illusion and if you follow these steps the two will fit together perfectly. Pin the pieces together at either end, exactly where the seam allowances will cross. Fold and finger-crease each piece to find the midpoint of the seams, then pin at the midpoint. Fold again to find the midpoint between this pin and the pins at either end of the seam. Pin. Make sure at all times that the cut edges of the two pieces line up exactly. Continue pinning until the fullness of the piece on top is eased in, then begin stitching. You will have a nice smooth curve.

DATE _____

DATE _____

"*American patchwork is lovelier far than its English counterpart because it was its makers' only outlet for the poetry and love of beauty pent up in their minds. At home in the Old Country the housewife had all the outlets of civilization; in New England she had only one, and that was her patchwork quilt. She made it—and all her life she was always making one more—because materials were so scarce that every scrap must be utilized; but she made it beautiful because there was no other beauty to be had in her log cabin home.*"

AGNES M. MIALL
*Patchwork Old and New*, 1937

.................................................................................................................................

.................................................................................................................................

.................................................................................................................................

.................................................................................................................................

.................................................................................................................................

.................................................................................................................................

.................................................................................................................................

.................................................................................................................................

.................................................................................................................................

## TIP

When cutting shapes from decorative fabrics such as border prints, preview the
finished design before you begin cutting. If, for instance, you plan to cut four border-
print triangles to sew up into a new square, begin by laying a triangle template on the
fabric, covering the portion of the design you plan to cut. Next, take two square mirrors
and position them along the two short sides of the triangle. Gently remove the
template, and the image in the mirror will show you how the finished piece will look
when it is sewn together.

DATE _____

DATE _____

*"The border should be considered from the beginning as part of the design, not added as a makeshift use for the pieces that are left over. . . . If the center pattern and the border have one distinctive thing in common, such as repeats of a motif or a definite combination of color, the design is united."*

AVERIL COLBY
*Patchwork Quilts*, 1965

...................................................................................................................................

...................................................................................................................................

...................................................................................................................................

...................................................................................................................................

...................................................................................................................................

...................................................................................................................................

...................................................................................................................................

...................................................................................................................................

## TIP

A common mistake when measuring for borders is to measure
along the *edges* of the quilt top, then cut accordingly. The
problem here is the outer edges usually have quite a bit of
stretch in them, so you will cut the borders longer than
necessary, resulting in a ruffled edge that will not lie flat. For
a true, accurate measurement, measure your quilt top
horizontally and vertically through the *middle* of the quilt.

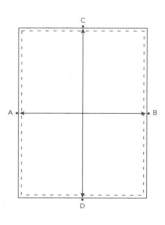

DATE _____

DATE _____

*"The [unbordered] quilt may be ever so much work, beautifully done, and yet look disappointingly ordinary when finished. I'd as soon hang my pictures unframed as to finish my quilts unbordered."*

RUBY SHORT MCKIM

*101 Patchwork Patterns*, 1931

## DATE _____

......................................................................................................................
......................................................................................................................
......................................................................................................................
......................................................................................................................
......................................................................................................................
......................................................................................................................
......................................................................................................................
......................................................................................................................
......................................................................................................................
......................................................................................
......................................................................
......................................................................
......................................................................
......................................................................
......................................................................
......................................................................
......................................................................
......................................................................

## TIP

If you plan to design and sew a pieced
border, it is important to take extreme care
when cutting the pieces. Make absolutely
sure that no bias edges fall on the edges of
the border, or there will be a tremendous
amount of stretching all along the border
edge, making it extremely difficult to sew
onto the quilt with accuracy.

DATE _____

DATE _____

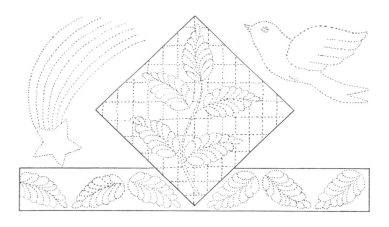

"To make a quilting frame, order from a lumber yard or sawmill four strips of hard pine 1 inch thick, 3 inches wide, and 6½ feet long. These could not cost more than twenty-five cents. Tack a piece of muslin along the edge of each strip. Buy four clamps for a dime at a hardware store, or have them made by a blacksmith, and you have a cheap set of frames that will last a lifetime."

SIDNEY MORSE

*Household Discoveries*, 1908

## DATE _____

..................................................................................................

..................................................................................................

..................................................................................................

..................................................................................................

..................................................................................................

..................................................................................................

..................................................................................................

..................................................................................................

..................................................................................................

..................................................................................................

## TIP

When quilting straight lines, I have an easy technique to avoid having to mark the quilt design on the fabric. I simply plan the design so that the width of the space between the lines is the same as the width of a strip of masking tape. I then stick the masking tape along the area to be quilted and stitch right next to it, along its length. When the stitching is done, I peel away the masking tape and it leaves no mark or residue at all.

DATE _____

DATE _____

"*Drawing round familiar objects secures many a wanted shape. For instance, pencil round plates, saucers, cups, egg-cups or coins for circles. For the slightly elongated diamond and for the heart—the latter wanted for Flirtation and often for quilting—buy a set of bridge sandwich cutters at the sixpenny stores and mark round the shapes required.*"

AGNES M. MIALL
*Patchwork Old and New, 1937*

DATE _____

....................................................................................................................................

....................................................................................................................................

....................................................................................................................................

....................................................................................................................................

....................................................................................................................................

....................................................................................................................................

TIP

To create the popular feather design for quilting, begin by drawing the *spine*—I usually choose a double line of stitching, about ¼" apart. Next, draw guidelines at the desired width on either side of the spine. Then use a coin or a button to draw half circles, side by side along the guidelines. Finally, a free-hand curved line will connect the half circles to the center spine.

DATE _____

DATE

*"Telling you how to quilt is almost as impossible to write in words as to describe an accordion without moving your hands. One quilter says use a short needle, another holds out for a long needle, nicely curved! After trying it and observing experts it seems to me that the trick is in sewing clear around and back again like your hand could roll around the small curved units, sort of a standing on your head effect. Aye, this is the rub that may keep the quilts of today form really rivaling the ones of yester-year."*

RUBY SHORT McKIM
*One Hundred and One Patchwork Patterns*, 1931

DATE _____

..........................................................................................................................

..........................................................................................................................

..........................................................................................................................

..........................................................................................................................

..........................................................................................................................

..........................................................................................................................

..........................................................................................................................

..........................................................................................................................

..........................................................................................................................

..........................................................................................................................

............................................................................

............................................................................

............................................................................

............................................................................

............................................................................

............................................................................

## TIP

Thin battings make quilting go faster.
They are smoother to quilt through and
make it easier to achieve small, even
quilting stitches. All-cotton battings are
less prone to *bearding*, or the migration
of fibers to the surface of the quilt.

DATE _____

DATE _____

"It will be a great pity if this lovely and traditional craft is allowed to die out, it is so typical of our country life. Of course, a large frame in a small house is very cumbersome, and it certainly is very trying to have to make the fingers so sore, but surely to create such lovely things it is worth while. In all the present-day hurry, it is restful to look back on the peaceful leisured workers who employed their spare time to such effort, and achieved such art, and who would be 'scumfished' [astonished] at the interest and wonder which their work arouses in the eyes of visitors . . . "

BEATRICE SCOTT
*The Craft of Quilting*, 1935

........................................................................................................................................

........................................................................................................................................

........................................................................................................................................

........................................................................................................................................

........................................................................................................................................

........................................................................................................................................

........................................................................................................................................

........................................................................................................................................

## TIP

It is easy to check to see if your stitches are too tight or too loose when the quilt is stretched in a frame. Insert the tip of a needle into one of the stitches and then try to pull up the thread a little. If you cannot even get the needle into a stitch, the tension is too tight. If you can pull up any excess thread, the stitches are too loose. Another way to check on the tension is to run a finger along a stitching line on the back side of the quilt. There is good tension if you can feel the ridge of the stitches. If you do not feel any stitches at all then the thread has not been pulled tight enough.

DATE _____

DATE _____

DATE _____

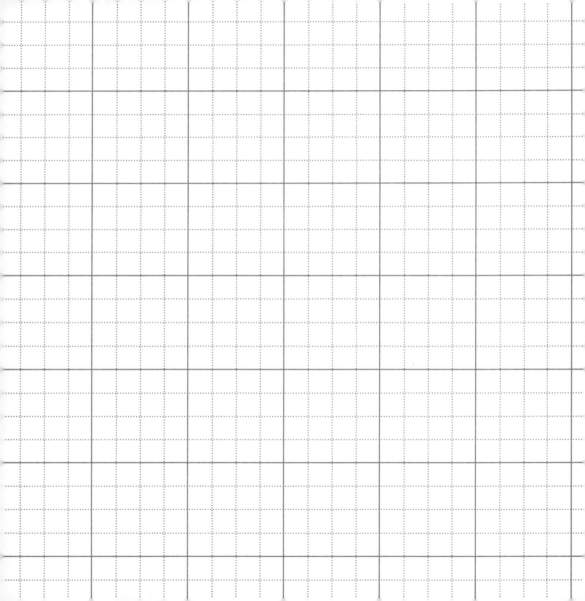

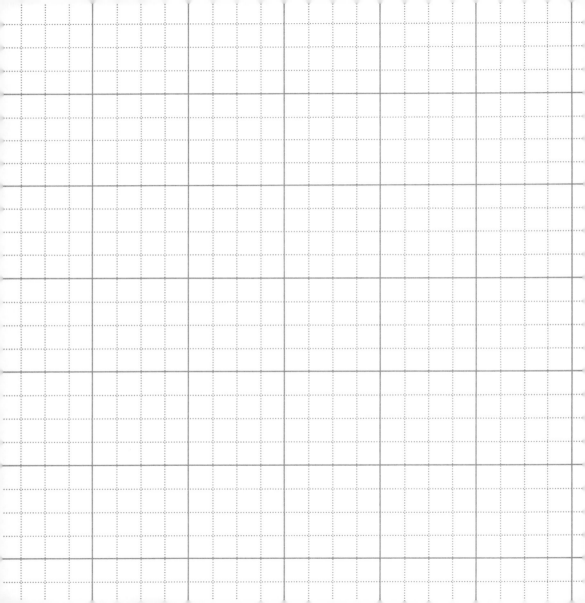

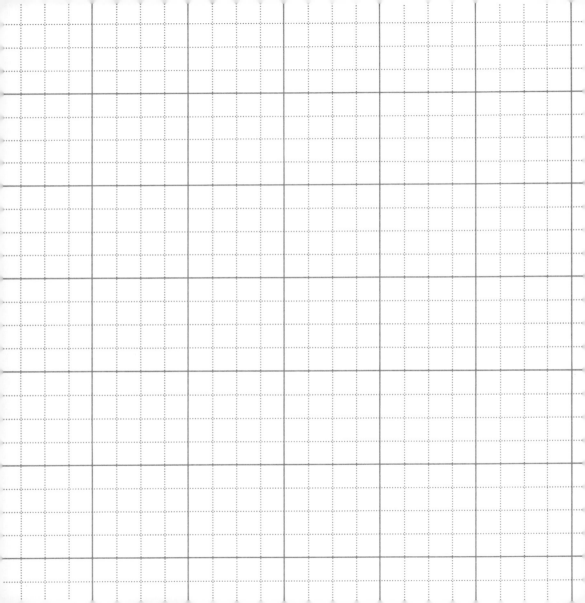

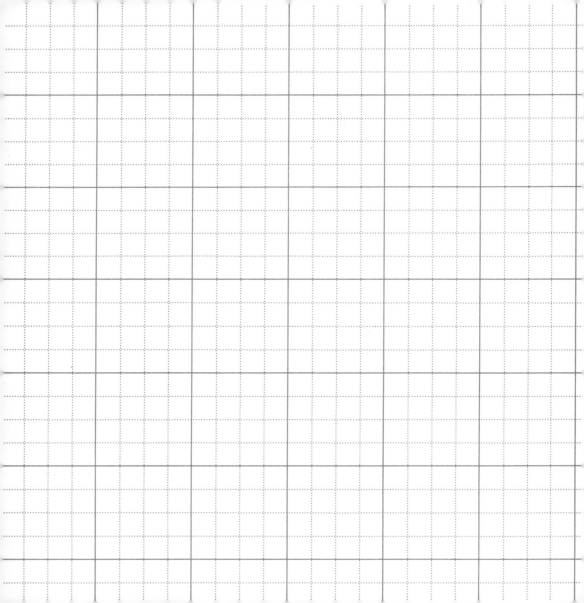

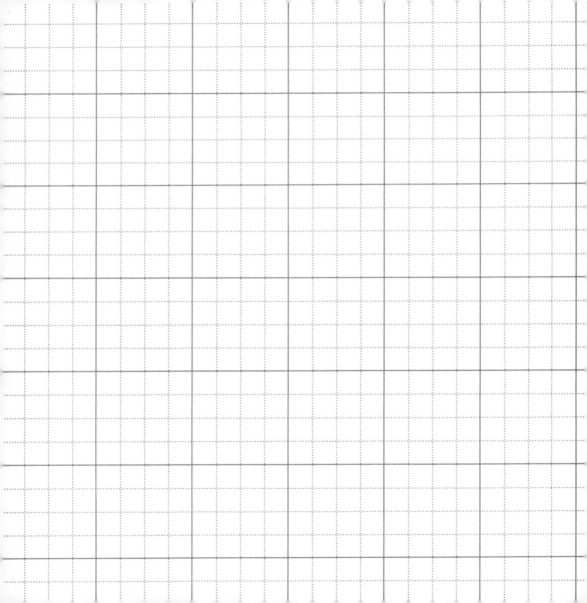

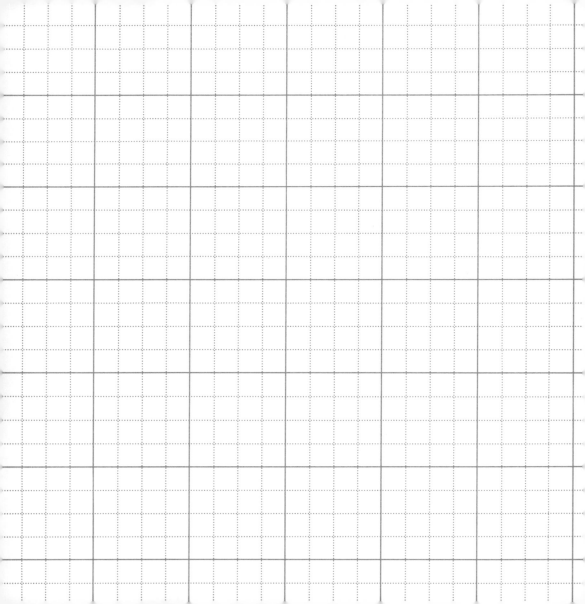

# Bibliography

Jinny Beyer, *Quiltmaking by Hand: Simple Stitches, Exquisite Quilts*, Breckling Press, Elmhurst (Chicago), 2004

*Cassell's Household Guide to Every Department of Practical Life: Being a Complete Encyclopaedia of Domestic and Social Economy*, Volumes I–IV, Cassell & Company, London, circa 1875

*Averil Colby, Patchwork Quilts*, Charles Scribner's Sons, Copenhagen, 1965

Therese de Dillmont, *Encyclopedia of Needlework*, Dolluf-MIEG & C, Mulhouse, Alsace, 1884. (Reprinted by Running Press, Philadelphia, 1996)

Ruth E. Finley, *Old Patchwork Quilts and Women Who Made Them*, J. B. Lippincott Company, Philadelphia, 1929

Jane Eayre Fryer, *The Mary Frances Sewing Book, Adventures Among the Thimble People*, The John C. Winston Co. Philadelphia, 1913

Carrie A. Hall and Rose G. Kretsinger, *The Romance of the Patchwork Quilt in America*, Caxton Printers, Caldwell, Idaho, 1935.

Rose Wilder Lane, *The Woman's Day Book of American Needlework*, Simon & Schuster, New York, 1963

Ruby Short McKim, *101 Patchwork Patterns* (1931), reprinted by Dover Publications, New York, 1962. Compiled from patterns produced by McKim Studios, Independence, MO, and related syndicated columns and booklets from the late 1920s and 1930s.

Agnes M. Miall, *Patchwork Old and New*, The Woman's Magazine Office, London, 1937

Sydney Morse, *Household Discoveries*, NY Success Company, New York, 1890

Beatrice Scott, *The Craft of Quilting*, The Dryad Press, Leicester, England, 1935

Marie D. Webster, *Quilts: Their Story & How to Make Them*, Tudor Publishing Company, New York, 1915

# About Jinny Beyer

JINNY BEYER BEGAN QUILTING in 1972 when she and her family lived in India and Nepal. Using her simple drafting system and inspired by the culture of the Far East, she created *Ray of Light*, a medallion quilt that won the top prize in the prestigious Great American Quilt Contest sponsored by Good Housekeeping and the U.S. Historical Society. The award catapulted her into the quilting spotlight where she began her career as a professional quilter, author, lecturer, teacher, fabric designer, and artist. Today, Jinny Beyer is one of the world's foremost quilters. She is the author of 12 books and three videos and, working with RJR Fabrics, has designed thousands of fabrics specifically for the quilt industry, including her signature border prints. She travels extensively throughout the U.S. and internationally, teaching workshops and giving lectures. Her annual seminar on Hilton Head Island in South Carolina is one of the most popular venues for quilters of all skill levels.

Jinny Beyer lives with her husband in a 250-year-old farm house in Great Falls, VA, just outside Washington, D.C. She pieces and quilts all of her work entirely by hand.

# *Also by Jinny Beyer*

*Quiltmaking by Hand: Simple Stiches, Exquisite Quilts*

*Jinny Beyer Perfect Piecer: A Multi-Angle Template for Piecing Perfect Points*

*Mystery Quilt Guide: A Resource for Teaching Quiltmaking by Hand*

*Patchwork Puzzle Balls: Quick-Sew Projects from Simple Shapes*

*Hand-Piecing with Jinny Beyer: A Video/CD Program for Quilters*

For more information, call 800 951 7836 or visit www.brecklingpress.com.

*"It took me more than twenty years, nearly twenty-five, I reckon, in the evening after supper when the children were all put to bed. My whole life is in that quilt. It scares me sometimes when I look at it. All my joys and all my sorrows are stitched into those little pieces. When I was proud of the boys and when I was down-right provoked and angry with them. . . . And John too. He was stitched into that quilt and all the thirty years we were married. Sometimes I loved [him] and sometimes I sat there hating him as I pieced the patches together. So they are all in that quilt, my hopes and my fears, my joys and sorrows, my loves and hates. I tremble sometimes when I remember what that quilt knows about me."*

AN UNKNOWN GREAT-GRANDMOTHER